Keep Them Calling!

Superior Service on the Telephone

Sherry L. Barrett

American Media Publishing
4900 University Avenue
West Des Moines, IA 50266-6769
800-262-2557

Keep Them Calling!
Superior Service on the Telephone

Sherry L. Barrett

Credits:

American Media Publishing:	Arthur Bauer
	Todd McDonald
	Esther Vanier
Project Manager:	Karen Massetti Miller
Designer:	Gayle O'Brien

Published by American Media Inc., 4900 University Avenue, West Des Moines, IA 50266-6769

Library of Congress Catalog Card Number 95-78189
Barrett, Sherry L.
Keep Them Calling! Superior Service on the Telephone

Printed in the United States of America, 1997
ISBN 1-884926-47-9

Introduction

Each time you use the phone at work, *you* become the company. That's the basic premise of this book. You represent your organization each time you pick up the telephone. How you represent your company defines your success on the job. When you're successful in your work, you also experience less stress, better pay, and more prestige. So, even though you are working for the company's success, when you deliver excellent customer service on the phone, you are enhancing your own well-being too.

You are reading this book for a reason. That reason may be reflected in one of the following objectives:

◆ To improve your comfort and confidence on the phone

◆ To use customer-service strategies that get results

◆ To enhance your professionalism and your company's image over the phone

Serving customers on the telephone may be 100 percent of your job. Or it may only be a small percentage of the work you do. But chances are good that it may be the single most important aspect of how you represent your company or organization. And remember, customer loyalty and satisfaction have the greatest impact on the success and longevity of your business.

About the Author

Sherry L. Barrett is a creative, results-oriented consultant, trainer, and speaker. She is president of Barrett Consulting, a human resources management consulting firm based in West Des Moines, Iowa. She provides professional services in the areas of communication, customer service, human resources, and management development. Her clients represent a broad range of public- and private-sector entities, to whom she brings the experience and insight gained from many years as an educator, manager, consultant, and volunteer.

Sherry Barrett earned a B.A. in English from Indiana University, followed by graduate degrees in education and leadership from Indiana University and Western Michigan University. An active member of the American Society for Training and Development, she sees her mission as helping others achieve their potential.

Lifelong learning is a joy to Sherry Barrett, and she hopes this book supports readers' professional development in a meaningful way. She welcomes comments and inquiries, which can be directed to her at Barrett Consulting, 512 45th Street, West Des Moines, Iowa 50265.

Acknowledgments

Sincere thanks to my colleagues for helping me critique and edit this book. Special thanks to Alysse, Lauren, and Tim for their constant patience, humor, and encouragement.

Self-Assessment

You have undoubtedly perfected many skills related to providing the best possible service for your customers or clients.

As you begin to read this book, it's helpful to have a goal in mind.

Use this brief self-assessment to honestly identify your successful service strategies and your areas of potential. You will get the best results from the self-assessment when you respond candidly and quickly.

1 = Seldom 3 = Sometimes 5 = Always

1. I know how to project myself positively on the telephone in a way that benefits both my organization and me.	1	2	3	4	5
2. I know how to stay positive even on the worst day.	1	2	3	4	5
3. I know how to give callers "touchy" information without irritating them.	1	2	3	4	5
4. I recognize customers' communication styles and adapt to them appropriately.	1	2	3	4	5
5. I'm comfortable using empathy statements to address callers' feelings.	1	2	3	4	5
6. I use mirroring to build trust and rapport with callers.	1	2	3	4	5
7. I know how to handle calls outside my area of expertise.	1	2	3	4	5

8.	I know what it costs my company to lose a customer.	1	2	3	4	5
9.	I know how to deny customers' requests tactfully and honestly.	1	2	3	4	5
10.	I know how to respond to two dimensions of a caller's anger.	1	2	3	4	5
11.	I know how to deal with an abusive caller.	1	2	3	4	5
12.	I open and close calls professionally.	1	2	3	4	5
13.	I extend an offer to help in my greeting.	1	2	3	4	5
14.	I know how to define customer-service excellence in my organization.	1	2	3	4	5
15.	I know how to keep a smile in my voice with each call.	1	2	3	4	5
16.	I ask callers whether they can hold.	1	2	3	4	5
17.	I use a formula for the voice-mail messages I leave.	1	2	3	4	5
18.	I always share as much information as possible.	1	2	3	4	5

19.	I feel confident and comfortable serving customers on the phone.	1	2	3	4	5
20.	I use blameless apologies to address customers' concerns.	1	2	3	4	5

Total your score. Find your score in the ranges below.

20–40 = You are interested in meeting customers' expectations, although you need work on the basics. This book will help you improve.

41–60 = You are beginning to realize your customer-service potential. Many of the techniques in this book will support your service success.

61–79 = You are using several techniques that are paying off well for customers. You can be more consistent.

80–100 = You are consistently using customer-service strategies that get positive results. You can fine-tune your service with some advanced techniques found in this book.

Circle the items you scored with a 3 or less. You can continue reading this book with a goal in mind to increase those numbers to 4s or 5s. Finally, make a commitment to continue using strategies that you rated as 4s and 5s. Now, let's move on!

Self-Assessment

Chapter*One*

Polishing Your Performance on the Telephone

Chapter Objectives

▶ Get ready to improve your customer service on the phone.

▶ Understand the five dimensions of customer service.

▶ Recognize your impact on the customer and the company.

Satisfying customers over the telephone is often more challenging than serving them face-to-face.

Y ou have remarkable potential to be a stand-out in delivering customer service on the telephone! You may currently be working on the phone as a routine part of your job, you may have just been hired in a position that is new to you, or you may have recently been transferred to a different position that requires telephone service. Regardless of your title, the reality is that the people who hired you believe in your service potential with customers on the telephone.

Your specific qualities, abilities, and experiences helped you get this job. Your interpersonal skills on the telephone will be critical in helping you keep it. Satisfying customers over the telephone is often more challenging than serving them face-to-face.

1

If you are a "seasoned" professional, you may be thinking, "I know what to do on the phone!" You are absolutely right! But think about your professional counterparts in sports. In baseball, for instance, the season starts every year with spring training. Rookies practice side by side with the most accomplished players. Each spring, every player reviews the basic skills and techniques that are the foundation of the game. The same is true for telephone service pros. A refresher of the basics, coupled with new information, can boost even the most experienced person into star-performer status.

> **Callers partner with you to get their needs met over the phone.**

As you know, the reasons people call you relate specifically to the particular type of work your organization does. Callers can be referred to as customers (internal and external), clients, patients, vendors, distributors, donors, members, guests, and associates. But no matter how you identify your constituents on the phone, they all have something in common. They become your telephone partners. They partner with you to get their needs met over the telephone.

Take a Moment

Think about how YOU use the telephone at work. Complete this overview of your impact on others on the telephone.

Why I Call Others
Identify the specific reasons that YOU call people during the workday.

Example: I call to order supplies and to request service on our copier when it's broken.

1. _____

2. _____

3. _____

4. _____

Why Others Call Me
Identify the specific reasons that people call you or your company.

Example: Customers call to place orders or check on an interest rate.

1. _____

2. _____

3. _____

4. _____

Basic Needs of Customers on the Telephone

Every call is an opportunity to enhance customer relations.

Our telephone partners may be customers, but they are people first. All callers have basic self-esteem needs that must be addressed on the telephone. As you read through these six needs, check those that are important to you when you call a company for a product or service.

♦ To be recognized and remembered

♦ To feel valued

♦ To feel appreciated

♦ To feel respected

♦ To feel understood

♦ To feel comfortable about a want or need

Take a Moment

Reflect on the quality of your current telephone partnerships by answering the following questions.

1. Do I anticipate or recognize all of my caller's needs?
    Always   Sometimes   Seldom

2. Do I ask whether there is anything else the caller wants or needs?
    Always   Sometimes   Seldom

3. Do I convey a clear message of valuing and respecting my caller?
    Always   Sometimes   Seldom

Use your answers to think about why you want to take your current customer service to a higher level.

Every telephone call is an opportunity—an opportunity to enhance customer relations and the image of your organization.

Why Improve?

Many people responsible for offering top-notch service on the telephone have never received specific training on what to do to get the best results. This book is a personalized learning opportunity to help you polish your performance on the telephone. If you are an experienced telephone service representative, it's an invitation to commit to using over 100 telephone tips in this book.

Motivation to make changes comes from within us. In polishing one's performance on the telephone, people are motivated by both work-related and personal benefits. Review the list to see whether these benefits are motivating you now. *Make a note to yourself if these fit for you.*

Personal Benefits

❏ **yes** ❏ **no** Does my customer service get recognized and rewarded now?

❏ **yes** ❏ **no** Do my current telephone service skills help reduce my stress in dealing with difficult calls?

❏ **yes** ❏ **no** Do I realize that my success on the telephone can translate to more sales commissions and/or chances to advance?

❏ **yes** ❏ **no** Do I feel personally satisfied when I'm doing a great job?

❏ **yes** ❏ **no** Do I recognize how important my role on the telephone is in maintaining and improving quality service in my organization?

1

People are motivated to polish their telephone performance by both work-related and personal benefits.

Company/Organization Benefits

❏ yes ❏ no Does my accurate and responsive telephone service save time in handling complaints and fixing errors?

❏ yes ❏ no Does my company save money when I promote services and products efficiently on the telephone?

❏ yes ❏ no Does keeping my current telephone partners happy save time, money, and effort in cultivating new customers? (Remember, it costs between five and six times more to *secure* a new customer than it does to *maintain* one.)

❏ yes ❏ no Do I enjoy being at work more when I feel like I am making an important, valuable contribution to the company and my customers on the telephone?

❏ yes ❏ no Do I build strong bonds with customers that enhance their loyalty? (That might contribute to your company's longevity and your job security too.)

Take a Moment

Identify the top two reasons that are motivating you now to polish your performance on the phone.

1. _____

   _____

2. _____

   _____

Keep these motivators in mind as you continue reading. Being motivated will certainly support your success in offering quality service on the telephone.

Five Dimensions of Customer Service on the Telephone

You know excellent customer service when you hear it. In fact, you can feel it over the telephone. The person on the other end of the line could be a salesperson, a receptionist, a customer service specialist, or a computer technician. The point is that each of us can deliver "knock your socks off" service on the phone if we know what to deliver.

What kind of telephone service do people value so highly? See if you agree with the five dimensions of service that create outstanding results with customers.

1. Professionalism

Professionalism is felt by callers when they are treated with courtesy and believe that the person they are talking with is competent. Professionalism comes through clearly when callers feel listened to, regardless of the requests or concerns they present. Professionals on the phone also control background noises for their telephone partners, such as chewing gum, clanking earrings, blaring radios, etc.

Professionalism is felt by callers when they are treated with courtesy and believe that the person they are talking with is competent.

DO:

◆ Use common courtesies such as "please" and "thank you."

◆ Listen objectively—regardless of the caller's concern.

◆ Control background noises.

◆ Demonstrate a "can do" attitude.

DON'T:

◆ Have a predetermined mindset about the caller.

◆ React negatively to the customer's problems.

◆ Use industry jargon.

◆ Get easily flustered, annoyed, or irritated.

2. Speedy Responses

Speedy responses are a key to excellent service. Who has extra time to kill? Nobody! Superior customer service comes through quickly, but never at the expense of quality.

DO:

♦ Get to the point as quickly as is appropriate.

♦ Change your voice message frequently (more than once a day).

♦ Predict how long a follow-up action is likely to take.

♦ Do what you say you're going to do—strengthen your follow-through and credibility with each transaction.

DON'T:

♦ "Pad" the conversation with idle chatter.

♦ Take more than 24 hours to return a call.

♦ Fail to call if a promised action is going to be delayed or impossible to take.

♦ Forget to follow through exactly on promised action.

3. Accurate Information

Accurate information saves time, tempers, and trouble. The best service is based on the best preparation. Callers know when they are dealing with the "expert" in any given situation. Callers understand important information more efficiently when they hear you speaking clearly and courteously.

DO:

♦ Continue to enhance your product expertise.

♦ Improve your telephone service by reading, attending training and meetings, or working with a "seasoned" in-house expert.

> Superior customer service comes through quickly, but never at the expense of quality.

- ◆ Use references in an efficient way.

- ◆ Use easy-to-understand examples and analogies to explain complex issues.

DON'T:

- ◆ Guess about critical information.

- ◆ Blame coworkers for errors.

- ◆ Use outdated materials as resources.

- ◆ Assume callers will understand your industry jargon.

4. Genuine Concern

Have you ever been reluctant to call with a question or concern because you didn't feel very comfortable with the issue? The best service representatives know how to extend genuine, sincere concern to the caller who has an enormous problem as well as to those with minor questions. Callers recognize when the service representative respects them as real people with legitimate issues and feelings.

> **Callers recognize when the service representative respects them as real people with legitimate issues and feelings.**

DO:

- ◆ Stay in control of your own emotions.

- ◆ Use empathy to reflect the caller's feelings and concerns.

- ◆ Realize that your customer's satisfaction is your success.

- ◆ Extend yourself to resolve difficult problems.

DON'T:

- ◆ Deal only with the task or technical problem.

- ◆ Show impatience.

- ◆ Judge the caller's feelings.

- ◆ Let one negative call "bleed" into the next one.

We'll talk more about difficult customers later.

5. Reliable Follow-Through

Reliable follow-through makes the difference between a very satisfactory service encounter and an annoying one. Following through on the customer's request is the most enduring memory of the service transaction. When follow-through is done well, the caller knows that you "walked the talk" and took care of his or her needs in a very concrete way.

DO:

♦ Accept personal responsibility for taking promised action.

♦ Enjoy the sense of achievement that comes when the follow-through is completed for the customer.

♦ Precisely what you promised as quickly as possible.

DON'T:

♦ Take incomplete or delayed action on a request.

♦ Blame others for errors or misperceptions—just do what needs to be done.

♦ Pass along responsibility without adequately preparing your coworker to take the necessary action.

Professionalism, speedy responses, accurate information, genuine concern, and reliable follow-through—these five dimensions of service generally describe the foundation of polished telephone performance in every organization. However, different companies have specific expectations about how they prefer to treat their customers on the telephone. Look through the list below and check off any resources that could help you better understand your organization's service expectations.

❏ Your company's mission statement

❏ Your supervisor

❏ Coworkers as service role models

❏ Your company's employee handbook

❏ Departmental training guides or trainers

❏ Other company resources (specify)

> **Reliable follow-through makes the difference between a very satisfactory service encounter and an annoying one.**

18

1

Take a Moment

Think of a time when you received outstanding telephone customer service. List three reasons that the level of service was remarkable.

Situation: _____

_____

_____

1. _____

_____

2. _____

_____

3. _____

_____

Would these same service strategies work with your calling customers? If so, how consistently are they used by others in your company? Could you use them more often?

Telephone Service and Competition

For many businesses, the telephone is their most important customer relations tool. In today's business environment, many companies offer similar products to the consumer at competitive prices. One of the ways businesses distinguish themselves in the marketplace is through the quality of service they offer to their customers.

The quality of your telephone service can directly affect your company's "bottom line."

One of your goals is to make yourself and your company stand out through exemplary telephone service. Keep in mind that the quality of the customer service you provide can have a direct impact on the "bottom line" of your company. Poor service is an invitation for customers to try your competition.

Never underestimate the impact you have on how your company is perceived. Who makes the difference? You do! You determine the level of customer service that your company or department is known for.

Building on the Basics

Think about the first telephone you used at home or at the office. Technology has changed telephone systems dramatically over the past 25 years. Technology changes, but the basics of excellent customer service do not. As you continue to work through this book, you will find that building on the basics of telephone service will give you the best possible results. Excellent customer service strategies are not only learned, but they are constantly reviewed and enhanced.

The chapters that follow will address these essential elements of professionalism on the telephone:

◆ Projecting a positive attitude on the phone

◆ Service techniques for opening and closing the call

◆ Handling customers on hold in a professional manner

◆ Effective ways to receive and leave voice mail messages

◆ Recognizing callers' various communication styles

◆ Developing rapport with callers

◆ Dealing appropriately with angry, upset, and abusive callers

◆ Handling difficult or out-of-the-ordinary situations

◆ Identifying and reaching goals for improving your telephone service

Yes, I Can!

Think about the useful ideas in this chapter. You're motivated to make improvements in the quality of your customer service. Jot down a message to yourself that reminds you why telephone service matters to you or your company.

Yes, the quality of my customer service on the telephone matters

because _____

_____

Chapter *Two*

Creating Positive Relationships on the Telephone

Chapter Objectives

▶ Understand how projecting yourself positively benefits you and the customer.

▶ Understand how to stay positive on the worst days.

▶ Choose the most constructive way to share information.

You're ready to begin improving your telephone service today. You may ask, "What do I do first?" Even in the dictionary, *attitude* comes before *service*. Let's start with the most fundamental component of customer service—your attitude.

A positive attitude is the engine that drives excellent service forward.

Your attitude colors every part of your relationship with your telephone partners. A positive attitude is the engine that drives excellent service forward. Imagine yourself calling Company XYZ for service on your car. Contrast the differences in these two responses to your service request on the telephone. Which customer service person would you prefer on the other end of your line?

■ A. "Yeah, this is Tony. No, I can't do that. Hold on. You'll have to talk to my manager."

■ B. "Good morning, XYZ Company, this is Tony. How can I help you today? (Pause) Yes, I can check with my manager about that. Would you like to hold, or would you prefer that I call you back in a few minutes with an answer?"

2

As a customer, you have undoubtedly experienced both good and bad telephone service. If we look behind the scenes, the difference becomes apparent. The person who provides genuine service has a positive, caring attitude that supports his or her telephone service skills. In a positive service relationship, customers know they are cared about from the beginning to the end of the conversation.

The person who provides service needs to have a positive attitude and truly care enough to provide the best service possible. Even the best technical phone skills won't help with a poor attitude.

The dictionary gives us some important clues about what constitutes a positive attitude. In the human context, *positive* means: "confident, certain, expressed definitely, real and affirmative." Has anyone described your attitude in those terms recently?

What are the advantages of having a positive attitude on the phone?

A positive attitude can:

◆ Reduce the potential for irritating the caller.

◆ Create goodwill with the caller.

◆ Lessen stress for you.

◆ Help you enjoy your job more.

◆ Help you do a better job.

◆ Create a better work environment.

23

Positive Attitudes Are Contagious

If you smile at someone, he or she usually smiles back. The same principle applies on the phone.

Callers recognize your positive attitude through your tone, rate of speech, and word choice. It's easier to start the call in a positive way. Then you are appealing to positive emotions rather than negative emotions. Negative emotions are hard to dispel once they get started. Positive emotions also motivate people to action more quickly.

People aren't born with a positive attitude. They create it. You have created a particular set of beliefs that guide the choices you make.

> The optimist proclaims that we live in the best of all possible worlds; and the pessimist fears this is true.
> Branch Cabell,
> *The Silver Stallion*

How to Develop and Keep a Positive Attitude

1. **Make a conscious choice to be positive.** Encourage yourself to see the benefits before you see the negatives in any situation.

2. **Link the outcomes of staying positive with a concrete consequence.** Common ways of recognizing a positive attitude in the workplace include paychecks, raises, promotions, special recognition, respect, and recommendations.

3. **Choose a role model who has a positive attitude.** Ask that person how he or she stays focused on the positive.

4. **Go public.** Tell others that you are working on being more positive. Ask others whom you trust for their support and feedback on your positive efforts.

5. **Start "plus" conversations with a group of coworkers.** Try structuring a ten-minute conversation on a break to lift everybody's spirits. Ask others to share work-related topics that are upbeat. No negative topics allowed!

6. **Set daily goals relating to specific behavior that supports a positive attitude.** For instance, challenge yourself to pleasantly greet everyone in the office before you begin work. You will recognize more of your positive behaviors if you're focused on a specific goal.

7. **Do more things that bring you joy—on and off the job.**

8. **Reward yourself in a specific and meaningful way when you recognize that you are using a positive attitude.** Your reward will remind you of the benefits of staying positive.

9. **Make a list of all the reasons why you care about your job and your customers.** Keep adding to your list as new reasons to care become clear to you.

Take a Moment

Think about other new steps you might take to rejuvenate the positive power in your attitude.

_____

_____

_____

_____

_____

Your Tone of Voice Communicates Attitude

Your telephone partners are listening to your attitude on the telephone. In fact, one of the most common ways to identify sincerity about service is by one's tone of voice. Research concludes that adults pay close attention to voice tone—sometimes even more than to the content of the message. It's imperative that you are aware of how your tone and word choice work together to create a picture on the telephone.

The smallest change in voice inflection and emphasis can create an enormous impact on the caller. Your tone of voice is one of your most valuable tools over the telephone. Ask a trusted coworker how you sound when you're on the phone. Or, better yet, periodically record yourself when working on the phone. Be certain that your tone reflects the high-quality service and the positive attitude you want to convey!

Take a Moment

Read aloud the sentences below. Emphasize the **CAPITALIZED** word in each sentence to illustrate how emphasis and tone change the meaning. Jot down any reactions you have as you vary your tone of voice.

Reactions

1. "May I **HELP** you?" _____

2. "May I help **YOU**?" _____

3. "**WHAT** was the order number?" _____

4. "What **WAS** the order number?" _____

5. "**WHEN** can you come in?" _____

6. "When **CAN** you come in?" _____

Staying Positive

Occasionally, events outside of our control affect us. We sometimes let our feelings about one situation influence how we react to the next event. Consider this situation:

■ You overslept because you have a screaming headache. You dress quickly for work and skip breakfast. Traffic makes you 15 minutes late. You rush in to find your manager taking calls at your workstation. She's taken a message from your brother, who asks that you return an emergency call immediately.

In the example above, how would you feel about your manager taking your calls in your cubicle? How would you feel about your brother calling about an emergency?

Remember that events don't cause feelings; we *choose* how we feel. You might have chosen to be upset about both situations. Or you could have been relieved that your manager was there to cover for you. You realize now that she understands your job better. Now you have a more common frame of reference for future discussions.

As for your brother's call, you could actually be elated. He has been out of touch with your family for five years. No matter what the emergency, you will have a chance to touch base with him now.

Feelings are choices. When we realize that, we can choose the most appropriate response even on the worst, most stressful day. Have you ever had a morning like that? Most of us have. How do you "flip the switch" and turn on the positive customer service on your next telephone call?

It's critically important that we stay positive. Our jobs and reputations depend on it. When we let the emotions from one event leak into the next, the caller suffers. It's not fair, it's not right, and it's certainly not supportive of good service. Check the ideas you can use to stay positive—even on the worst day.

2

> Events don't cause feelings; we *choose* how we feel.

Staying Positive—Even on the Worst Day!

1. **Remember that feelings are a choice.** You control your choices.

2. **Realize that your feelings are separate from the work you need to do.** You can tell yourself that at lunch or after work, you will focus on resolving your personal problems. Until then, challenge yourself to perform in a way that leaves the customer out of your personal dilemmas.

3. **Take three deep breaths before you get back on the phone.** The extra oxygen will energize you, and exhaling should help reduce your physical tension too. You will probably be less likely to sigh on your next call. (Sighing usually communicates distress of some type.)

4. **Take five minutes to write down whatever is bothering you.** Fold it and put it away in a drawer. Set a time later in the day to respond to the concerns you wrote down.

5. **Focus on your caller's needs instead of your own.** Tell yourself, "I'm responsible for my customer's needs right now."

6. **Take a 30-second memory vacation.** Focus on a very pleasant vacation or activity that brings you joy. Come back from the minitrip more relaxed and refreshed.

7. **Think about a positive service role model.** Ask yourself, "How would this person handle this situation in order to stay positive?"

Take a Moment

Think about the steps you can take to do your job with a more positive attitude. What will you work on this week?

_____

_____

_____

_____

_____

2

The Case of Fractured Service

Case Study

■ Glenda has just transferred to Customer Service at the Boston Warehouse. She wanted to move to a customer service position from accounting. The pay is much better, and the hours are shorter. Because she is partial to numbers, however, Glenda is a little worried about her ability to work well with people on the phone.

As she adjusts to her new role, Glenda finds that she still likes the predictability of her invoicing much better than the variety of requests she receives from customers. She is having a hard time believing that satisfying customers "counts" as an accomplishment if it doesn't translate into an order.

Glenda has been overheard answering the phone by saying, "Boston Warehouse—do you want to place an order?" However, most of the calls she gets are service-oriented questions, not requests for orders. Glenda's desk is full of file folders and papers to file. She is visibly flustered when she is on a call and can't find the appropriate references.

Glenda sits down with her best friend at lunch. Exasperated, she says, "Maybe I'll never be a good customer service representative on the telephone. All day long, people call and interrupt my work. And half the time, they're complaining about something I can't do anything about. I'll never have time to get my real work done! What am I to do?"

Glenda is not representing herself or the company in the most positive and professional way.

Glenda is not representing herself or the company in the most positive and professional way. Take a look at the suggestions for maintaining a positive attitude earlier in this chapter. If you were Glenda's best friend at work, what could you recommend to help her create a better attitude and improve her customer service on the phone?

_____

_____

_____

_____

_____

_____

_____

Read the author's notes that follow for some other ideas to improve Glenda's telephone service and her attitude.

Author's Ideas

1. Glenda could create a "balance sheet" listing the advantages and frustrations of the new position. She could share her frustrations and potential solutions with her new manager. Glenda has to make a choice to provide excellent customer service in all aspects of her job. Without that conscious choice, her negative attitude will bleed through every call.

2

2. Glenda needs to understand that meeting customers' needs *is* her job. She needs help to move from a very task-oriented position to one in which interpersonal skills count as much as completing an invoice.

> Glenda needs help to move from a very task-oriented position to one in which interpersonal skills count as much as completing an invoice.

3. Glenda needs to develop a positive greeting on the phone that includes offering to help the caller. A better greeting might be, "Good morning. Boston Warehouse. This is Glenda in Customer Service. How may I help you this morning?"

4. Glenda needs to rearrange her work space in order to get organized and reduce distractions. The filing needs to be done periodically so she can access current information in the files with ease. An experienced coworker might share some valuable tips on storing reference materials to ensure that they can be easily accessed during a call.

5. Glenda needs to keep a pad of scratch paper and a pen handy so she can jot down the caller's name. She needs to use the caller's name at least once during the call.

6. Glenda can take advantage of the slowest part of the day to complete the majority of her invoices. She may be able to arrange coverage with a coworker to ensure that calls are being handled while one person does paperwork.

Making all of these improvements should reduce Glenda's frustrations on the telephone, help her focus on the caller's needs, and may give her more time to devote to the product invoices that she enjoys the most.

Creating Positive Impressions

You're more aware now of how staying positive creates a favorable service relationship. You control how the caller perceives you and your organization. It only takes seconds to make an impression—positive or negative. And one word can tell a tale.

Word choice seems simple, but small changes make a dramatic difference. Some words trigger emotions in our telephone partners. We have the opportunity to shape those responses by the words we use. Negative phrasing or word choice sets the caller up to react defensively. Positive phrasing, on the other hand, creates a service climate in which the caller can more easily respond with an open mind.

Take a Moment

Rewrite the following negative statements to create a more positive relationship with your telephone partners. (Hint: Using a *"when you . . . we will be glad to . . . "* formula works well to get the customer's compliance or action on an issue.)

Example:
"You have to complete the application before we can do anything."

"*When you* have completed the application, *we will be glad to* process it immediately."

1. "Your file must be lost."

_____

2. "I'm going on lunch break, so I'll do it later."

_____

Take a Moment *(continued)*

3. "That's not my job."

_____

4. "She's not in yet."

_____

5. "Hold on a minute."

_____

6. "I'm not trained on that. You'll have to talk to Tom."

_____

7. "We never received your order."

_____

8. "We're too busy to do any rush orders now."

_____

9. "It's a computer problem."

_____

We sometimes fall into habits that prevent us from communicating positively with callers. Use your rewrites of the negative phrases above to change a negative communication habit into a positive one. You will be pleasantly surprised when you encounter more cooperative people on the other end of the line!

Compare your answers with the author's suggestions on page 94.

2

Packing Great Service in "Cans"

A "can do" attitude gets results with customers. One powerful way to put a "can do" attitude into action is by eliminating "can't" from our vocabulary. If you were to ask, "How is great service packaged?" the answer would be, "In CANS!"

"I can't" ranks high on the list of "trigger" words that annoy customers. Close seconds are "You have to," "No," and "It's our policy."

Take a Moment

Read the examples to hear how the *"I can't"* in each message has been stated as a positive *"can do"* statement.

Examples:

"I can't get this in the mail until tomorrow."

"I can mail this in the morning."

"I can't read the signature on this application."

"I can see that the application is signed, but it's difficult to read!"

Identify two reasons why you may be unable to provide service or product to a customer.

Reason #1: _____

_____

Reason #2: _____

_____

Now go back and write a "can do" statement that you can use in these situations.

Striking *"I can't"* and *"we can't"* from your service vocabulary isn't difficult. It does, however, require your sincere effort to change a familiar communication habit.

Denying Customers' Requests Tactfully

Customers call with a specific need in mind. They want a particular outcome. You're obviously concerned about providing excellent service. There will be times, however, when it is impossible to grant a customer's request. Read on to discover a technique that can help you enhance the service relationship and still deny a request.

2

The "sandwich" technique layers the "bad" news in between two pieces of "good" news. In the same way you build an appetizing sandwich, you can create an appealing message that allows the caller to hear the refusal more objectively.

"Good news" opener	Start positive. Use positive words, not negative words. Thanking the caller for asking the question is a positive beginning. Or stating that you're glad to offer an explanation gets the conversation moving in a positive direction. "I can" statements and empathy can be useful here too.
"Bad news" middle	Be honest and specific. Apologies are usually well received. Be careful if you speak about a company policy that limits your ability to respond to a customer's request. Frame the policy around a specific benefit to the caller, not to the company.
"Good news" closing	End on a positive note with some type of goodwill message. Emphasize positive words again. "Even though we were unable to help you this time, we would be glad to work with you in the future."

35

Take a Moment

Identify the three parts of the sandwich technique used in this example. Match the paragraphs below to the appropriate description.

1.   "Good news" opener _____

2.   "Bad news" middle _____

3.   "Good news" closing _____

Situation: The caller is speaking to an auto mechanic about a transmission repair that he believes is covered under a warranty.

A.   It is true that your warranty covers repairs to your transmission. We would be glad to repair the transmission. As I have explained, the warranty has expired, so you will be responsible for the cost of the repairs. I have a used transmission in stock now that could save you about 50 percent of the cost of the repair. How would you like to proceed to get your car running as soon as possible?

B.   Thank you for asking about your manufacturer's warranty. I'd be glad to explain the situation to you.

C.   Unfortunately, your warranty expired two days before you brought your car into the shop.

Check your answers with the author's on page 94.

The Sandwich Technique: A Case Study

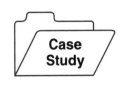
Case Study

■ Starting and ending on a positive note increases your chances of resolving the caller's problem despite your denial of his or her request. Read the following conversation between a corporate relations representative and a salesperson in which the "sandwich" technique is used. As you read, identify the three parts of the sandwich technique.

2

Situation: A sales representative calls the Corporate Office to request that his commission check be issued on Wednesday instead of Friday. The request must be denied.

Corporate Relations Representative:
Hello, this is Pat in Corporate Relations. How may I help you?

Caller:
This is Tom Smith, Pat. I need to ask a favor. I hope you can help.

Corporate Relations Representative:
We would be glad to try, Tom. What is it that I can help you with today?

Caller:
My sales commission check. I've got some urgent financial demands. I need my check Wednesday instead of Friday this week.

Corporate Relations Representative (using the sandwich technique):
We can process your commission check on the last two sales accounts that we received last Friday, Tom. Those were for $7,500 and $3,200, respectively. Unfortunately, we're not able to guarantee the production of your commission check any earlier than 10:00 a.m. on Friday.

What I can do is request that your check be delivered the same day by Federal Express. There would be a small additional charge, but they guarantee delivery by 2:00 p.m. in your area.

Take a Moment

Identify a typical request that you may need to refuse in your organization.

_____

_____

Write a denial using the sandwich technique.

_____

_____

_____

_____

_____

Using the sandwich technique creates an opportunity for the caller to hear "bad" news more easily. You may find it helpful to write out some sample scripts for yourself that address common requests that must be denied. After you practice using the sandwich technique at work, you'll be surprised at how helpful it can be in other arenas of your life.

Yes, I Can!

Think about the useful ideas in this chapter. Staying positive pays premium dividends for you and the caller. Great service relationships increase profits and boost confidence. Jot down one way that you create positive relationships on the phone with every customer.

2

I create positive relationships on the phone when I _____

_____

_____

_____

Chapter *Three*

The Basics Work!

Chapter Objectives

▶ Handle all transfers effectively.

▶ Efficiently manage the three parts of every call.

▶ Create a positive image of yourself and the company on the telephone.

You have fewer than five seconds to get a call started on a positive note.

Y ou've taken the first step to excellent customer service on the telephone by creating and maintaining a positive attitude. In this chapter, you'll learn more specific techniques about managing the three distinct parts of a telephone call. Those three parts are the opening, the body, and the closing.

Time is precious in a service situation. Telephone service professionals know that they have fewer than five seconds to get the call started on a positive note. Read on to discover the best way to navigate efficiently toward your customer's satisfaction on the telephone.

Opening the Call

We all make instantaneous judgments about a company or a person by the way we are greeted on the phone. If we have been waiting for the phone to be answered for more than three rings, we begin to get impatient. Then, if the person answering the phone sounds hurried, rude, or disinterested, the call is tainted even more. Beginnings are powerful. Check yourself to see if you are making the most of them.

Prepare in Advance

3

Your attitude shows through in every telephone contact. Make sure before you pick up the phone that you're approaching the call in the most positive way.

Support your positive phone style by organizing your work space. If you're using a computer, make sure you are ready to input on the appropriate screen. Always keep paper and pencil handy to jot down pertinent information during the call.

In addition, have any references that you may need to use during the call within arm's reach so you can avoid putting the caller on hold while you locate your materials.

Smile Through the Phone

Keep a "smile in your voice." Adults pay more attention to the tone of your voice than they do to the words you use. It's so important to excellent service to sound upbeat and enthusiastic about the chance to speak with the caller.

How do you keep smiling for every telephone partner? Here are some tips from customer service professionals on staying cheerful call after call.

How to Keep a Smile in Your Voice

1. **Post a small mirror by your telephone.** Look at yourself speaking on the phone. Force a smile even if you don't see one. Eventually, your brain will catch up to your facial muscles and you will actually begin to feel more cheerful. It's hard to sound unpleasant when your face is smiling.

2. **Write yourself a note and tape it to your telephone or on your computer monitor.** Challenge yourself to smile for every caller. (Some people find it helpful to "keep score" of their smiling success on a pad of paper by the phone.)

3. **Ask your coworkers to support you on the phone by giving you feedback.** Ask them to gently remind you when you slip into a neutral or negative tone of voice. Be sure to use this arrangement to give each other positive feedback every day too!

4. **Practice a telephone greeting with someone you trust and respect.** Force yourself to be as exuberant as possible, and ask for reactions from your trusted listener. You may even want to record it so you can hear yourself from the caller's point of view.

5. **Tell yourself that the next caller is a favorite person with whom you have been waiting to speak for a long time.** Your high energy and sincerity will make the person feel like he or she *is* very special to your organization. And how can that hurt business?

6. **Stand up when you feel low on energy.** Answer the next call on your feet and with a smile on your face.

It's hard
to sound
unpleasant
when your
face is smiling.

Answer Promptly

Answer by the third ring. You let callers know that you respect their time and have a sense of urgency about handling their calls when you pick up calls quickly.

If you can't answer promptly, make sure to arrange coverage of your telephone by a coworker who is willing and able to accept your telephone calls. It's critically important to *ask* coworkers if they can provide coverage for you before forwarding your calls to them. A surprised or harried coworker may inadvertently create a negative impression when he or she answers the phone for you.

Answer by the third ring.

3

If you have a message feature on your telephone, and you find that the outgoing message has begun before you've been able to answer the call, do pick up the call. Don't just listen to the message and then call back. It is appropriate to pick up the call, identify yourself, and apologize for not being able to pick up the call more quickly. Then simply ask, "How may I help you?" and begin the conversation.

Greet the Caller and Identify Yourself

Greet the caller by saying, "Hello," "Good morning," or by stating the name of your company. If you do not receive calls directly on outside lines, chances are the caller has already heard the name of your company.

Callers want to know the person with whom they are dealing.

Identify yourself just after the greeting. In many cases, your first name along with the name of the department (where appropriate) will suffice. Callers want to know the person with whom they are dealing. A simple, "Hello, this is Tim in Marketing" sets a positive tone.

Offer to Help

Capitalize on the positive by asking, "How may I help you?" It almost seems too simple to matter. But that simple offer pays big dividends when callers realize that you are ready to assist them. You help them focus and articulate their purpose when you offer to help at the beginning of the call.

Avoid "Blind" Transfers

Frequently, you will greet the caller and find that he or she desires to speak with another person. Handling the transfer professionally is one of the hallmarks of outstanding telephone skills.

Handling the transfer professionally is one of the hallmarks of outstanding telephone skills.

Have you ever closed your eyes and been led from room to room in a business asking for the person to whom you wanted to speak? Probably not. But you can imagine that some callers feel like they've had that experience when they have been blindly transferred over and over.

"Blind" transfers, when the caller gets transferred to an unknown party, decrease your effectiveness with the caller. People simply don't like being shuffled from person to person in a service situation. Being transferred without any notion of whom you will speak to next is frustrating at the least. Blind transfers leave the caller feeling lost in the phone system.

Remember, people call with a purpose. Their goal is to express that purpose and get some action taken on it.

The following suggestions can eliminate the caller's frustration with being transferred blindly and can increase your company's image in the process.

How to Avoid "Blind" Transfers

1. **Ask the caller whether he or she *can* hold, or offer to take a message.** Say, "Would you mind holding, please, while I transfer you to _____?"

2. **Tell the caller to whom they're being transferred.** Say, "I'm going to transfer you to Pat Smites now at extension 1234." Or, if the call will be directed to a call distribution center, tell the caller the name of the department.

3. **Stay on the line until your coworker responds to the transferred call.**

4. **Briefly introduce the caller to the coworker.** Say, "Pat, I have Jan Morales on the phone with a request for a rush shipment."

5. **If a coworker is unavailable, ask the caller if you can take a message or if someone else can help, or ask if he or she prefers to leave a message in voice mail (if available).** Say, "I'm sorry, Pat is on another line. May I take a message, or would you prefer to leave a personal message in her voice mail?"

Following these important steps will lead your telephone partner calmly and directly to the response they called to get.

3

Managing the Body of the Call

Check yourself on the key service strategies in the middle or body of every phone conversation. In this section, we will briefly review listening and reacting to the caller's needs, and putting callers on hold. All of these basic components add up to exemplary service that works on the telephone!

Listen Carefully and Enthusiastically

Give your customer your complete attention. Limit distractions. Have a pencil and paper handy, or use your computer to capture important information. Listen to every need the caller expresses. Make brief notes while you listen to keep focused. And key points of the call will serve as a useful checklist when you close the call.

Give your customer your complete attention.

Use the Caller's Name

Nothing sounds sweeter than our own name. The best salespeople know that this principle builds rapport. Use the caller's name at least once in the conversation whenever possible. (Using the caller's name more than three times can tune some people out.) Personalizing the contact tells the caller that you are paying close attention and are tailoring your response to him or her.

Respond to the Caller's Need or Request

Be enthusiastic and concerned when you react to the specific needs or requests the caller shares. Use "I can" language to inform the caller about the action you will take. Demonstrate your expertise with confidence, and you'll send a clear message that your company can respond and that the caller is valued.

Ask the Customer to Hold

One of the most common errors in telephone customer service is the failure to ask callers *if* they are *able* to hold. So often, we assume that because they are on the line, they are both willing and able to hold.

How to Put a Caller on Hold

1. **Always ask the caller *if* he or she can hold.** Sometimes a caller won't want to hold but would prefer to call later or to be called back.

Always ask the caller if he or she can hold.

Do say . . .	Don't say . . .
"Would you like to hold?"	"Hang on a minute."
"Could you please hold while I look this up for you?"	"Hold on while I look this up."
"Would you like to continue holding, or could I call you back when I have the information?"	"You will have to continue holding."

2. **Explain why you need to put the caller on hold.** A simple, brief explanation helps relax callers and makes them aware that you are working for them while they wait.

Always check back with the caller in 30-second intervals.

3. **Always check back with the caller in 30-second intervals.** Being put on hold without any consistent contact makes the caller wonder whether you have forgotten him or her. Over the phone, a caller does not have the advantage of seeing or hearing you as you separate from him or her even for a few seconds.

4. **If your phone system doesn't have a timer, be sure that you have a clock or watch with a second hand close by.** The shorter the holding period, the more positive the interaction will be with the caller.

First and last impressions are powerful. Review the best of the basics in closing a call positively and professionally.

Closing the Call

Repeat the Action You Agreed to Take

Clarify by summarizing the actions that you and your telephone partner have agreed upon. By offering a summary statement to your caller, you create the perfect opportunity to eliminate any confusion or misunderstanding.

Close the Call Formally

Summarize the actions that you and your telephone partner have agreed upon.

Equally important to the best opening is the close, or ending, of a call. Callers remember the final few seconds of the service transaction. It's important to leave a positive feeling when you close the call.

You may thank them for calling and then say, "Good-bye." The formality of this type of ending says again to the caller, "I respect you." Try to let the caller hang up his or her receiver first.

Say "Good-Bye" Instead of "Bye-Bye"

Many of us have the habit of saying "bye-bye" to end a call. While this is better than simply hanging up, it is not as desirable as the more professional sounding "good-bye." If you're a "bye-bye" person on the phone, set a goal for yourself to end the conversation on a more professional note. You may choose to say "good-bye" instead of "bye-bye." Or close by saying, "Thanks for calling. I'll talk to you next Tuesday." When you eliminate the "bye-bye" from your telephone vocabulary, you'll be replacing one communication habit with a better one.

Most of us know what works with customers on the phone. Sometimes we get busy or distracted and forget a critical step in ensuring the customer's satisfaction. You might find it helpful to copy the following review of key points in creating a positive service relationship with your telephone partner. Use it as you monitor yourself during your next ten calls. You will be surprised by what you discover. The basics really do work!

Telephone-Service Basics Did I . . .	Yes	No
1. Answer promptly?	_____	_____
2. Greet the caller and identify myself?	_____	_____
3. Offer to help?	_____	_____
4. Listen carefully and enthusiastically?	_____	_____
5. Use the caller's name?	_____	_____
6. Respond to the caller's need or request?	_____	_____
7. Clarify and summarize the key points that we agreed upon?	_____	_____
8. Close the call formally?	_____	_____
9. Say "good-bye" or "thanks for calling" instead of "bye-bye"?	_____	_____

3

Yes, I Can!

Think about the useful information in this chapter. Write a positive message to yourself about how you create positive impressions by the way you manage the basics of opening or closing the call.

Yes, I can _____

_____

Chapter *Four*

Communicating with Style

Chapter Objectives

▶ Recognize four common communication styles.

▶ Build rapport by recognizing the customer's communication style.

▶ Build trust by mirroring the customer's words, rate of speech, and tone.

▶ Learn how to use empathy to enhance your relationships on the phone.

I n most cases, you only have one chance to make a favorable impression on a customer. Research shows that the more callers feel "connected" to you, the higher the probability that they will trust you. Trust and rapport with a caller helps us get moving in a positive direction to meet that caller's needs.

The more callers feel "connected" to you, the higher the probability that they will trust you.

Four skills help us build rapport with the caller:

1. An ability to recognize the customer's communication style.

2. The willingness to adapt our approach to meet his or her needs.

3. Knowledge of how to mirror back the caller's tone, words, and rate of speech.

4. A willingness to address the customer's feelings using empathy statements and blameless apologies to build trust with the customer.

Communication Styles Differ

People tend to behave in fairly predictable ways on the telephone. Studies of communication behavior identify four basic ways people relate on the phone. The four types of communication styles people use most often are:

1. Expression-oriented

2. Relationship-oriented

3. Detail-oriented

4. Results-oriented

You may be familiar with these four dimensions of behavioral style—but you may know them under different labels. Labels you may have heard include:

4

♦ Analytical, amiable, driver, expressive

♦ Cautious, steady, dominant, influencing

♦ Owl, dove, eagle, peacock

Remember that the label is not as important as the personal style that it represents. To be as effective as possible, you need to know two things about communication styles on the phone:

1. Your style

2. The caller's style

To understand your style and the style of your telephone customers, let's look at each of the four styles more carefully.

Expression-oriented: Enjoys talking, likes people, and expresses feelings openly.

■ "Everyone in our department loved the idea. It's going to be fantastic working with all different departments, isn't it? I'm so excited I can hardly wait to get started. Think of all the new things we'll learn by sharing ideas with each other."

| Relationship-oriented: | Prefers predictable outcomes, values cooperation and collaboration. |

■ "We are really comfortable working with you. You have given us the best possible service in the past. We are counting on a long relationship that is mutually beneficial."

| Detail-oriented: | Prefers facts, data, and specifics. Wants to understand how and why something is done. Wants to cover the fine points. Values accuracy and precise information. |

■ "I'd like to know exactly how long it will take me to become proficient on this new software. If I go through the tutorial first, which section of the user's guide should I begin with? Is there anyone else who has upgraded to this software whom I could talk to about problems they might have encountered in the transition?"

| Results-oriented: | Prefers focusing on the results, or "bottom line." Likes speedy responses focused on results, not the process. Straightforward in asking for what is needed. |

■ "I need refreshments for 50 people tomorrow at 5:00 p.m. Have your people make the menu appealing to people over 70. I want it all set up, served, and cleaned up by your staff. All I want to have to do is show up and enjoy my guests."

Which do you think you are?

❏ Expression-oriented

❏ Relationship-oriented

❏ Detail-oriented

❏ Results-oriented

Take a Moment

Match the appropriate description with the correct communication style.

E = Expression-oriented   **D = Detail-oriented**

R = Results-oriented   **RL = Relationship-oriented**

1. ____ Would appreciate the briefest possible conversation.

2. ____ Might say, "I just love the way you've remodeled your store."

3. ____ Is organized in their thinking, likes details and procedures outlined.

4. ____ Might say, "I don't care how you do it, just get me three temporary staff members who can hit the ground running."

5. ____ Expresses feelings about events and people freely, asks for your opinion.

6. ____ Might say, "On our team, we always compare our results to see how we might help each other get the best group outcome."

7. ____ Speaks directly to the point, doesn't want to "beat around the bush."

8. ____ Values predictable outcomes and likes to include others in collaborating on projects and decisions.

Check your answers with the author's on page 94.

Understanding communication styles gives you an important tool for relating to the caller quickly and effectively. As the telephone-service professional, it's up to you to modify your approach to meet each caller's need. Your best communication style is "flexible," so you can adapt to any of the four styles your callers use.

Build rapport with your caller by using his or her preferred style to transact business.

How to Adapt to the Caller's Communication Style

First, make a decision to tune in to the customer. When you use your best listening skills, you will hear definite clues about your telephone partner's style and how he or she prefers to be treated.

The strategy is straightforward. Listen to identify the caller's style. Adapt or flex your style to meet the caller's needs. When you do, you will build rapport with the caller by using his or her preferred style to transact business.

Use the chart on the following page to see this process in action.

Listen to the Caller's Conversation	Identify the Caller's Communication Style	Create Your Rapport-Building Response
1. "Everyone loved the idea . . . "	**Expression-Oriented:** chatty, enthusiastic, varied tone of voice; faster-paced speech	Respond with feeling words and enthusiasm about the idea.
2. "Exactly how long will it take me to . . . "	**Detail-Oriented:** speaks precisely, asks "how, why, when, where" questions to get key issues covered	Tell them immediately exactly how long the process should take; offer any details about experience that will back up the validity of your estimate.
3. "I need refreshments tomorrow for 50 people . . . "	**Results-Oriented:** states needs and wants directly; very little emotion stated	Respond quickly that you can meet the stated need; hit the high points quickly and don't get bogged down with details about how you will do the work.
4. "I'm counting on a long relationship . . . "	**Relationship-Oriented:** talks about cooperation and prefers predictable outcomes	Express the value of a trusting, long-term relationship to you; reinforce your commitment to cooperative efforts that will continue to give them good results.

4

It is your responsibility to adapt or flex your style to meet the needs of the caller. If you are an expression-oriented communicator talking with a results-oriented customer, sparks could fly! You need to be aware of when to shift gears to relate, using the customer's preferred style.

Which of these responses demonstrates that the service representative is adapting to the customer's style on the phone?

Customer using an expression-oriented communication style:

- "I'd be thrilled to be able to get this delivered yet today. It's a super-special occasion, and I know my fiancé will just flip when he finds out what I've arranged."

Service representative responding:
- ❏ A. "The order has been input on our DLV system. Order number 678TMN will be delivered at 4:00 p.m. Central Standard Time."

- ❏ B. "Wow! He really will be surprised when we deliver this by 4:00 today. Thanks for letting us help you with this fantastic gift!"

Response B is an excellent example of the service representative's adapting her style to the caller's expression-oriented style. This professional captured the emotion and enthusiasm the caller was feeling. Connecting with the caller's style will increase the chance that the customer will do business with this person in the future.

Customer using a relationship-oriented communication style:

- "We wanted to do something rather low-key to celebrate the team's completion of this project. We were just wondering if your company might have some suggestions that our team could review? We've never done anything like this, so we're a little out of our league. That's why the committee wanted to get your ideas about how to do this so everyone will be comfortable."

Service representative responding:
- ❏ A. "I'm sure that anything you come up with would work. Just let your imagination take control. You'll probably design the best celebration your company has ever had."

❏ B. "The team will really appreciate your efforts to recognize their accomplishments. Our company has planned events like this for the past eight years. We could suggest some low-key approaches for your committee to consider. Would you prefer to have the suggestions in writing, or would you like one of our senior consultants to meet with your group?"

Response B is the better choice. The service representative uses a slower pace to get to the information. The representative stresses the experience her group has had in planning similar events, which would appeal to this person's desire for stability. The final offer to send a senior consultant reassures the client about the seriousness of the request and the desired level of expertise.

4

Customer using a detail-oriented communication style:

■ "I have never ordered from your company before. What exactly do I need to do to set up an account? How will I be billed? What is involved in the approval process? What advantages are there to being a 'gold customer' when it comes to multiple orders?"

Service representative responding:
❏ A. "As a new customer, I know it's important for you to understand the precise way our service department works. Let's start from the beginning, and I'll be glad to explain each step of the process. I'm interested in your questions too."

❏ B. "The bottom line is that you get faster service as a 'gold customer' account. Why don't you fax the application in to see if you'll be approved before we get into a lot of nitty-gritty detail?"

Response A is a better example of the service professional paying close attention to the caller's high need for accuracy, predictability, and precision. Remember that callers want to know that you care about their needs and issues just as much as you care about their orders.

> Customer using a results-oriented communication style:

■ "I don't care how you process checks down there. I need a printout of my statement, and I need it now. Fax it to me at this number in the next 15 minutes, or I'm calling the bank president!"

Service representative responding:

❏ A. "I have to get my supervisor's approval and then take her written okay over to the accounting department. If she signs the authorization, I'll ask accounting to fax the statement to you as soon as possible."

❏ B. "Let me work on it, sir. If you don't receive the fax in the next 10 minutes, please call back and ask for me, Alysse Barkel, at extention 512."

Results-oriented communicators don't care *how* you arrive at the result, they just want the final outcome. Response B is the better choice because the service representative moves toward the caller's goal as quickly and directly as possible. Some results-oriented callers may sound abrupt or even rude, but they are really just concerned with the task at hand.

Building Rapport Through Mirroring

Now that you have a working understanding of callers' communication styles and how you can adapt to them, read on to discover another communication tool.

Studies show that the more "in sync" a customer feels with the service representative, the easier it is to build trust. A sophisticated communication technique called *mirroring* is a way to help the customer identify with you quickly.

Mirroring can be done in three different ways. You can mirror the customer's tone of voice, rate of speech, and words or phrases. Let's explore each type of mirroring in more detail.

Mirroring Tone of Voice

People vary their tone of voice depending on how they are feeling. When someone is agitated or excited, his or her tone may be higher and the volume louder. To mirror the caller's tone of voice, respond professionally by varying your tone to match hers or his. For example, if an elderly caller is on the line requesting an explanation about an investment, demonstrate concern and caring by the tone of your voice. Her investment may be her life's "nest egg," and she could be understandably concerned about how it is handled.

A student who has just been accepted into the college of his choice would have a great deal of excitement and enthusiasm in his voice. An appropriate telephone service response would also be delivered in a higher, congratulatory tone of voice, perhaps mixed with some humor.

The exception to the rule in mirroring relates to dealing with an angry caller. It's appropriate to match the pace or speed at which the person is speaking, but avoid mirroring the tone or content. When the caller calms down, make sure you slow your pace too.

> **You can mirror the customer's tone of voice, rate of speech, and words or phrases.**

4

> **It's appropriate to match the pace or speed at which the person is speaking, but avoid mirroring the tone or content.**

Mirroring Rate of Speech

Fast-paced speakers usually prefer a fast-paced response. Slower-speaking customers would be put off by a rapidly delivered explanation. Match the customer's rate of speech without being obvious. Subtle mirroring is appreciated when it isn't obvious to the caller. Callers feel more in sync as a result of your flexibility and effort.

Match the customer's rate of speech without being obvious.

Mirroring Words and Phrases

The most important thing to remember about mirroring is that it is not "parroting" back exactly what the speaker says. If the caller clears her throat, don't clear yours! If a caller is telling you how he or she feels, very carefully choose a few key words to mirror back in your response. If the caller feels that you are simply repeating what he or she said, the rapport will be damaged.

The most important thing to remember about mirroring is that it is not "parroting" back exactly what the speaker says.

Mirroring Example

Caller:
"I am so frustrated with these constant *repairs.* Why in the world do I have to *waste so much time harping* on you people to get the *job done right?"*

Customer Service Representative:
I certainly am sorry that you have had these recurring problems, sir. Please don't think that you are *harping* because our intention truly is to get the *job done right* for you. I don't want to *waste another minute* of your time. I will come out myself and *make the repair* this morning to resolve this problem immediately."

Take a Moment

Underline key words and then write a response that you could mirror back to the callers in these situations.

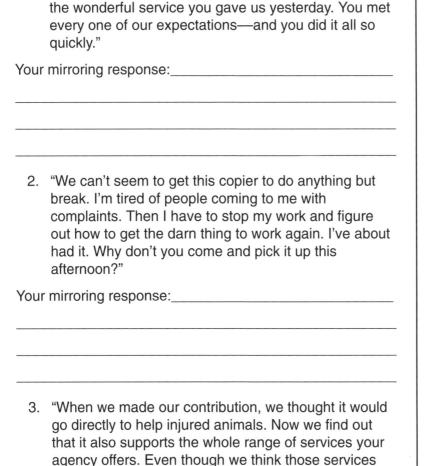

1. "I'm just calling to tell you how delighted we are with the wonderful service you gave us yesterday. You met every one of our expectations—and you did it all so quickly."

Your mirroring response:_____

_____

_____

_____

2. "We can't seem to get this copier to do anything but break. I'm tired of people coming to me with complaints. Then I have to stop my work and figure out how to get the darn thing to work again. I've about had it. Why don't you come and pick it up this afternoon?"

Your mirroring response:_____

_____

_____

_____

3. "When we made our contribution, we thought it would go directly to help injured animals. Now we find out that it also supports the whole range of services your agency offers. Even though we think those services are valuable, we feel deceived by the letter we got. I want a guarantee that our money is going to go specifically to help the injured animals."

Your mirroring response:_____

_____

_____

Check the author's suggestions on page 95.

4

Building Rapport by Empathizing

So far, you have explored the value of building relationships through a positive attitude, upbeat tone of voice, appropriate "can do" word choice, and sandwiching denials. There is another powerful skill to add to your repertoire—empathizing.

Empathy is an effective tool to let the caller know that you recognize his or her concerns.

You've undoubtedly heard about the benefits of empathy before. You have likely benefited from an empathetic response that someone shared with you after you expressed a concern. How can a technique like empathy work to improve your relationships with callers?

Regardless of the organization, callers will have concerns to express. Each caller wants to know that you care about his or her particular problem. Empathy is an effective tool to let the caller know that you recognize his or her concerns. According to the dictionary, empathy is

> *Understanding so intimate that the feelings, thoughts, and motives of one are readily comprehended by another*
> **or**
> *The capacity for experiencing as one's own the feelings of another*

Responding with empathy builds trust and rapport with the caller. Trust and rapport build strong relationships. To use empathy effectively, you must genuinely communicate that you recognize the caller's feelings. Empathy is not sympathy or feeling sorry for someone else. It is a way of communicating respect for someone else's perceptions, feelings, and life experiences. *You do not have to agree with the caller's perspective on a given issue to be empathetic.* You simply need to understand that whatever the person is feeling is real for him or her.

Using "Feelings" Words to Express Empathy

Effective empathetic responses are driven by "feelings" words. Some people misunderstand empathetic statements to simply be, "I understand how you feel."

Imagine a young woman calling a legal services clinic to express concern over eviction from her apartment.

Caller:
"I just can't believe what the landlord did. He knew that I was waiting for my unemployment check. I got laid off when the plant closed down last Tuesday. I gave him half of the rent, and he promised it would not be a problem if I gave him the other half when my check arrived. It came today. He threw all of my belongings out on the lawn. I don't know what to do."

Do you think this young woman would feel understood if the person she called simply said, "I understand how you feel"? Probably not. More empathetic responses would include:

■ "You're really shocked that the landlord went back on his word."

■ "It sounds like you're at a loss about what to do with the landlord and your belongings right now."

■ "You seem to have experienced a lot of difficult situations in the last two weeks. I can see how all of this would be very upsetting."

Empathy statements are specific. They include some reference to one of four typical emotions.

mad   sad   glad   afraid

Actually, no one can truly understand how someone else feels. In using empathy, we make assumptions based on the situation and what the caller shares with us. A meaningful empathy statement goes further to state the feeling you believe the person is experiencing.

4

Powerful empathy statements identify a specific feeling, even if you're not 100 percent sure what the caller is expressing. Take the risk to reflect back a feeling—the caller will either confirm that feeling or tell you more accurately what he or she is experiencing.

Take a Moment

Take a moment to underline the words that express feeling in the following empathy statements.

1. "I understand how frustrating it can be to wait for your check."

2. "I can see why you feel that way. It can be really irritating to call several times without getting a call back."

3. "I'd feel angry, too, if I didn't get the material I had specifically requested."

4. "It must be frightening to have that happen to you."

5. "It sounds as if you're upset about what your agent told you today."

6. "I hear the sadness in your voice."

Check your answers with the author's on page 95.

Hearing and reflecting back the caller's feelings are the keys to effective empathy.

Hearing and reflecting back the caller's feelings are the keys to effective empathy. Remember that empathy is *more* than simply saying, "I understand." Powerful empathy statements specifically identify the feeling the caller is expressing directly or indirectly.

Empathy and Blameless Apologies

Negative situations call for positive responses. Occasionally, an error—whether real or perceived—will come to your attention from a customer. In these situations, try blending an empathy statement with an apology. Empathy statements are often preceded or followed by a sincere, brief apology. In some organizations, apologies are seldom used over the phone. Apologies are avoided because the person using them erroneously feels that they are accepting blame for a condition they did not cause.

Enter the blameless apology. The blameless apology does not place the blame on anyone. It does reassure the caller that you believe they are upset or annoyed by a perceived error. Using apologies signals that you are paying close attention to what he or she is concerned about. It *does* reassure the caller that you care enough to listen further and to help resolve his or her concern.

4

Blaming Statements	Helpful Blameless Apologies
"I'm sorry, but you didn't send it in on time."	"I'm sorry that the deadline expired before we received your request."
"I'm sorry that Lauren didn't get this sent to you on time."	"I'm sorry that you have been inconvenienced by this."
"I'm sorry that Lisa told you the wrong way to get here."	"I'm sorry about the apparent miscommunication."

Customers will sometimes blame you for an error. It's tempting to "pass the buck." Never blame another person in your organization for an error. Blaming others never makes you look better. Instead, use blameless apologies and empathy statements, then resolve the problem.

Take a Moment

Which of these apologies could be used with your callers?

❏ "I'm sorry that you feel that way."

❏ "I'm sorry that happened."

❏ "I'm sorry that you have been inconvenienced by this."

❏ "I'm sorry that hasn't reached you."

❏ "I'm sorry about the apparent miscommunication."

❏ "I apologize for keeping you on hold. Now, how may I help you?"

You're right! All of these blameless apologies can work in almost any situation to let the caller know that you are concerned about his or her issue or problem. Blameless apologies are usually easier for customer service people to use on the telephone because they realize that they are not actually admitting that they are responsible for a perceived error. Remember, though, you also build credibility and trust when you apologize directly *if* your organization has made a mistake.

When you respond to the caller's frustration with empathy and respect, you demonstrate caring professionalism. Dealing with feelings first frees you up to get on to the "real" problem. You will find more tips on resolving callers' problems in Chapter 6.

Callers want to partner with us for service. A telephone partnership is one in which the caller is treated in a way that enhances rapport, loyalty, and good feelings. As a telephone professional, you can build trust and create positive connections by mirroring the customer's tone, words, and rate of speech. And the more you adapt to the caller's preferred communication style, the more effectively and efficiently you manage the call. Challenge yourself to develop the best rapport possible with every telephone partner!

Yes, I Can!

4

Customers trust us when they believe that we are like them and understand how they feel. Write yourself a positive message about the way you communicate understanding and trust to the caller.

Yes, customers trust me when I _____

_____

_____

Chapter *Five*

The Ins and Outs of Voice Messaging

Chapter Objectives

► Use a formula to create effective voice messages.

► Use a strategy to get your calls returned.

► Create a positive impression on voice mail.

Y our professional presence counts "live" over the phone and electronically on voice-messaging technology. Who could have predicted ten years ago how much we would depend on electronic processing of messages through voice mail? Everybody has an opinion about the advantages and disadvantages of voice mail. Regardless of how we feel about voice messaging, it's a reality.

Despite the technology, you still represent your organization with every recorded message.

Voice mail is a two-faceted dimension of telephone service. You leave voice messages for others, and you respond to messages left by your callers. Both dimensions require awareness of how to get the best results. Keep in mind that despite the technology, you still represent your organization with every recorded message.

Have you ever considered how much time you could save for yourself and others by leaving effective voice mail messages? The savings could be substantial! Consider how efficient your voice mail messages are as you read these guidelines.

How to Leave Efficient Voice Mail Messages

Think about a typical day on the telephone. How often do you reach the person you're calling the first time—10, 20, or 30 percent of the time? You can expect to *not* reach the person you're calling more often than you would prefer. When offered the chance to leave a voice message, take it. Your voice message is the next best thing to speaking directly to your partner. You remain in control of the details of the message, and your unique style comes through directly.

> **Your voice message is the next best thing to speaking directly to your partner.**

1. **Keep your message short and to the point, while sounding pleasant and courteous.** Use a greeting such as "Hello" or "Good morning."

   - State your full name and your company or department.

   - State the reason for your call. Request any specific action the caller could take before calling you back. You may need to include a reference to a specific client's name, policy, product, or invoice number. Never just say, "Call me back."

   - State your phone or extension number. Suggest the best time to call you back.

2. **If you must leave a long message, let the person know up front.** This gives the person a chance to save the message until he or she can give it full attention. Don't ramble. Use 30 seconds or less. Everyone has time constraints.

3. **If you are leaving a message with more than one point or request for action, state this at the beginning of the message.** Suggest that the person get a pencil and pad.

4. **Close messages with a courteous "Thank you," "Thank you in advance," or "Good-bye."** Remember that you are speaking to a customer, and good phone manners count on a recorded message too.

5. **Record on your calender any follow-up you need to do.**

5

69

Copy this form and use it to prepare for voice-mail messages.

Voice-Mail Checklist: 30-second message format

❏ Simple opening or greeting

❏ My name, company, and/or department

❏ Reason for the call

❏ Any specific information that is necessary to take action

❏ Specific request for action

❏ My phone number and extension

❏ Best time to call back

❏ "Good-bye" or "thank you" as a closing

❏ Note on your calender any follow-up you need to do

■ **A professional voice mail message might sound like this:**
Hello, this is Merrill Owens. I'm calling to request a certified copy of my birth certificate. I will fax a copy of my driver's license to you at this number before noon. I would like you to charge the cost to my USExpress account #222-555-999, expiration 2/99. You can reach me after 5:00 today, and tomorrow at 317-888-7896 if you have questions. Thanks for your help. Good-bye."

(Note the amount of numeric detail in this message. Remember to speak slowly when leaving precise data such as product numbers, phone numbers, and addresses.)

Take a Moment

Write a typical example of a message you frequently need to leave for someone else. Use the format outlined for a 30-second voice-mail message.

_____

_____

_____

_____

_____

Messages That Promote Action

If you are in a customer service or sales position, it may be helpful to leave a slightly different type of message for clients. You want them to call back so you can offer a product or service. Check out these tips for getting a higher rate of returned calls.

◆ **Explain a deadline for receiving a particularly attractive service or product.** You might say, "I have a 30 percent discount available on your supplies for the next 48 hours. Please call to take advantage of this extraordinary offer."

◆ **Describe new information that you can offer with a clear sense of importance or urgency.** Your message may include, "Please call for a critical update that will impact how we complete the next phase of the project."

◆ **Offer a product or service at no cost, if possible.** Your message could be, "If you can return my call today, I'll mail you a free copy of our best-selling book."

◆ **Use humor, but do it with caution.** Any humor should be free of potentially offensive language related to gender, age, disability, race, and ethnic background. You could say, "I had one of the funniest experiences in my sales career this week. Call me back, and I guarantee it will brighten your day."

5

71

◆ **Identify what you can do if you receive the return call quickly.** Try a message like, "If you can confirm your order by phone before 10:00 a.m. tomorrow, I will be able to ship it by noon."

◆ **Experiment with your closing techniques.** Use them in your voice mail messages. Keep track of which messages get the best response.

Quality customer service on the telephone depends both on sending and receiving voice mail messages. The way you handle incoming messages can mean the difference between average and superior customer service.

How to Create an Effective Voice Mail Greeting

The content of your outgoing message will encourage the caller to speak to you even in your absence.

Leaving an informative and personable greeting on your telephone extension is critically important. The content of your outgoing message will encourage the caller to speak to you even in your absence. The following ideas are key to a quality message.

◆ **Sound cheerful!** Don't you dislike hearing a bored or grumpy-sounding message when you get voice mail? Practice an enthusiastic greeting before you record it.

◆ **State your name clearly.** Speak slowly and distinctly.

◆ **Give pertinent information about your availability:**
   • When you'll be back
   • Who else the caller can speak with and how to access them

◆ **Give callers the option to bypass your gretting if they need to call later that day.** ("Press 2 if you want to skip my message the next time you call.")

◆ **Call your extension and listen to your message.** If it doesn't sound upbeat, clear, and informative, record it again.

◆ **If you are unavailable to retrieve messages, say so.**

◆ **Give callers the option to return to an operator or a coworker.** ("Press 0 and the # sign to be transfered to my assistant, Patsy.")

Tips for Handling Incoming Voice Mail

Incoming voice mail messages are a daily experience for most of us. Check these key ideas to see how professionally you are managing your incoming messages.

◆ **Listen with a pad and pen in hand.**

◆ **Listen to the complete voice-mail message.** Vital information is often presented at the end of the message.

◆ **Always return voice mail messages within 24 hours of the time the message was left.**

◆ **Clear your voice mail at least twice each day.** Set aside a time or times each day to listen and respond to messages. Keep notes for critical follow-up if you are unable to connect with the caller.

Voice messaging is here to stay! Clear, planned, outgoing messages communicate organization and professionalism. Speedy, thorough handling of incoming messages reinforces your commitment to services. Use the technology to your constant advantage—to communicate the best about yourself and your organization.

Yes, I Can!

Voice messaging is the next best thing to speaking with your customer directly. Think about how you can create a positive impact with the voice messages you leave for others.

Yes, when I leave a message, I can _____

_____

_____

5

Chapter *Six*

Responding to the Angry or Upset Caller

Chapter Objectives

▶ Recognize the impact of one unsatisfied customer.

▶ Recognize two problems of every irate caller.

▶ Use a method for addressing the upset caller's problems.

▶ Understand how to handle an abusive caller.

Y ou've been a customer thousands of times in person and over the phone. You know that the quality of expected customer service is defined by the customer. But what do callers really want when they are dissatisfied? Read on! This chapter will give you a clear idea about the best way to respond when your telephone partner is angry or upset.

Let's look at customers' behavior when they feel mistreated. A study of consumer complaints done by Technical Assistance Research Inc. demonstrates what customers do after a poor service transaction.

1. In the average business, for each customer who complains, there are 26 who feel the same way and don't speak up.

2. The customer who feels poorly served will tell between 8 and 16 people about his or her negative experience.

3. Businesses lose 91 percent of his or her unhappy customers to their competition.

4. It costs about five times more to attract a new customer than it does to keep a current one.

With the dramatic ripple effect of poor service, how many upset or angry customer errors can your organization afford in a month or a year?

There is good news. Your ability and willingness to handle conflict with customers can actually increase their loyalty to you. Between 82 and 95 percent of complaining customers will continue to do business with you if they feel you have remedied their complaint in a satisfactory way. Remember, your customers' satisfaction is *your* success.

> **Your ability and willingness to handle conflict with customers can actually increase their loyalty to you.**

Viewing Complaints as Valuable Information

As service-minded professionals, we often think of complaints or upset customers as the most negative part of our jobs. Actually, you can look at complaints as a gift! If your customers don't point out what isn't working for them, then who will give you that valuable feedback? Every organization needs to learn about how it is meeting the customers' needs. Complaints are a very direct way to get critically important information about changes you may need to consider.

There are strategies that work well when dealing with upset callers. Before you read about those strategies, think about your own experience in providing service to an upset or angry customer on the phone.

6

Recognizing Signs of Anger on the Telephone

When a customer calls with a serious problem, it doesn't take long to recognize the signs of anger over the phone. Check the behaviors you've recognized that tip you off to an angry caller.

❏ Higher-pitched speech

❏ Louder volume

❏ Long pauses

❏ Sighs

❏ Swearing

❏ Condescending tone

❏ Demands

❏ Threats to take business elsewhere

❏ Short, terse answers

You may have checked every item on this list. Each of these descriptions can signal an angry or upset caller. The first thing you need to do is tell yourself, "This anger is not directed at me personally." Remember that you represent your organization on every call you take. It's necessary to remind yourself that you are not the target of the caller's anger. When you keep your perspective service-oriented, you're able to manage the caller's frustration and his or her problem more effectively.

Read on to learn more about what to do when you suspect that the caller is quite upset or extremely angry.

Recognizing the Angry Caller's Problems

Your angry or upset caller is actually one person with two problems. The caller has:

1. A relationship problem with the company.

2. A specific problem that needs attention.

Deal with Feelings First

You realize that the angry caller has two problems. Which part of the problem needs attention first?

The first problem, although rarely stated directly, is that your company's relationship with the customer is broken. You begin to "fix" the relationship by dealing with the caller's feelings first. If you jump into solving the problem, the caller is unlikely to feel satisfied with any alternative, because she or he is still emotional about unmet relationship needs.

Very often, anger appears when customers' basic human needs are not satisfied. You will recall that the basic human needs of customers include a desire to feel:

6

◆ Recognized and remembered.

◆ Valued.

◆ Appreciated.

◆ Respected.

◆ Understood.

◆ Comfortable asking for what they want or need on the telephone.

Part I—Resolving the Relationship Side of the Problem

How do you step in to deal with the relationship needs of the angry caller? Imagine the caller's anger as a very full red balloon—almost ready to burst from the tension of the air inside it. If you use strategies to calm the person's feelings, the balloon full of emotion begins to deflate. The more the caller talks at the beginning, the faster the balloon empties. The caller becomes more open to problem solving as emotions subside.

Deal with the caller's feelings first.

How to Resolve the Relationship Problem

Use these steps to help reduce the caller's emotions and address the relationship that feels "broken" to the customer.

1. Deal with the caller's feelings first. The caller needs a chance to unleash emotion before getting down to solving a particular problem. Do this by listening without saying much or interrupting until the caller slows down or stops talking. Subtle ways of letting the caller know you're still listening include, "Yes," "I see," and "Go on."

2. Ask open-ended questions to encourage the caller to talk about his or her feelings in the situation. Don't defend your position or the company's policies. Just listen and take notes.

3. When the caller has answered all of your questions and has calmed down, summarize the caller's problem. Restate the main problems you heard. Ask for confirmation that you've identified the main issues.

4. Give the caller feedback about his or her concerns. Use empathy and blameless apologies to reconnect the relationship with the customer. You'll recall that empathy includes stating the feeling you heard the caller express either directly or indirectly. Blameless apologies express regret that the person has been inconvenienced or troubled in some specific way.

How to Ask Open-Ended Questions

Open-ended questions require more thoughtful and complete answers than "yes" or "no." Use open-ended questions when you want to encourage the caller to share ideas and feelings with you.

Open-ended questions start with:

Why?	*"Why did you decide to enroll at this center?"*
When?	*"When did you begin to feel the most agitated?"*
What?	*"What happened just before the injury occurred?"*
How?	*"How do you update your inventory?"*
Tell me . . .	*"Tell me how you believe this situation got out of hand."*
Could you explain?	*"Could you please explain to me the sequence of events that led to your current situation?"*

Use open-ended questions when you want to encourage the caller to share ideas and feelings with you.

6

Putting open-ended questions into your customer service tool kit will help you find out what the caller is thinking and feeling. Using open-ended questions can give you a chance to hear enough detail to be able to move toward resolving the "real" problem that needs attention.

Part II—Fixing the Problem

Now you're ready to "fix" the problem. Of course, you don't literally break the conversation into two parts. But in your mind, and with your actions, you do respond differently to the two dimensions of the caller's problem—the broken relationship and the "real" problem.

After you have helped the caller calm down emotionally, you can then move to the second part of the conversation: the caller still has a problem that needs attention. This second type of problem is usually related to a perceived error by the company or an employee. It could relate to a product or service that was either poorly delivered, misrepresented, or unnecessary.

Callers may want a credit on an invoice, a new widget for a broken one, a letter of apology for poor service, or a free appointment. The specific content of the problem will relate directly to your type of business and the caller's perception of what is wrong.

At this point, the caller is less emotional. It's only at this point that a rational, problem-solving approach will work.

How to Resolve the "Real" Problem

Use these steps to help resolve the caller's problem with the company in a way that will retain him or her as a customer.

1. **You have already responded to the relationship dimension of the problem.** You have listened carefully and responded with empathy.

2. **Begin to increase your speaking rate from a slower, concerned rate to a more active, energetic pace.** Start asking closed questions that help you answer the questions you have about the specifics of the complaint.

   Closed questions can be answered "yes" or "no." They can also be answered with facts, figures, and data. By switching to closed questions, you move from the open discussion of feelings to a more narrow focus about the details of the problematic situation.

   > **Offer the caller a choice of alternatives to resolve the problem.**

3. **When you feel that you have a clear understanding of the issues, restate them to get the caller's agreement about how you have defined the problem.** If the caller agrees, begin to offer alternatives to the customer. If the caller doesn't agree, ask more questions for clarification.

4. **Offer the caller a choice of alternatives to resolve the problem.** Be prepared to follow through on any of the alternatives that you suggest to your telephone partner.

5. **Let the *customer* decide which of the alternatives is best suited to his or her situation.** Restate the chosen alternative to get the customer's agreement.

6. **Follow through on what you agree to do.**

7. **With your manager's approval, do something extra whenever possible.** Adding some type of unexpected service makes your company seem extraordinary.

6

Often, a small, sincere gesture goes a long way toward maintaining a customer's loyalty. In your organization, what would be an appropriate way to show an angry customer that you want to keep his or her business? What "extra" service could you provide when you follow through on the solution? Some companies offer:

◆ Free shipping and handling on a product.

◆ Free samples.

◆ Faxing forms instead of mailing forms.

◆ Priority mailing or handling.

◆ Personalized processing of follow-up action.

◆ A note or letter of apology.

◆ A coupon or voucher for discounted or free service.

Take a Moment

List some of your own ideas for extra service your company could offer.

_____

_____

_____

Skillfully navigating a customer through his or her anger to the resolution of a problem is challenging. When you think about the customer really being one person with two separate problems, it's easier to remember to deal with both of the caller's needs. To briefly review, let's combine both parts of the caller's problem into one formula for handling the angry caller.

Seven Steps for Resolving the Irate Customer's Problem

1. Deal with the caller's emotions first. Listen carefully and respond with empathy.

2. Ask questions to get specifics about the complaint.

3. Restate the issues to get the caller's agreement.

4. Offer a choice of alternatives to fix the problem.

5. Let the customer decide which alternative to use.

6. Follow through on what you agree to do.

7. When possible, do something extra.

Post this list by your telephone. Being mentally prepared to deal with the angry or upset customer will increase your chances of quickly restoring the customer's faith in your organization.

6

Handling Abusive Callers

Nobody likes them, but everybody gets an abusive caller once in a while. We're talking about those callers who go beyond the predictable anger or frustration of some callers. Verbal abuse often includes swearing and accusations about a person's competence or personality. Verbally abusive callers go beyond appropriately expressing their anger about a problem and begin to attack the person handling the call.

Verbally abusive callers begin to attack the person handling the call.

Your company certainly does not expect you to be verbally abused over the telephone. In most organizations, you will be asked to use your own judgment to determine when a caller crosses the line and becomes abusive. Ask your manager to define what your company considers abuse on the telephone.

How to Handle Abusive Callers

We all have different tolerance levels for verbal abuse. Follow this four-step procedure when you feel you have a verbally abusive caller on the line.

Step 1

Stay calm. Tell yourself, "I am not the target."

Step 2

Give the caller a warning. You need to stay on the line long enough to speak to the caller about his or her behavior.

> **Never hang up without first giving the caller a chance to "cool down."**

Never hang up without first giving the caller a chance to "cool down" or improve his or her language.

Sometimes simply saying, "I beg your pardon?" may alert the caller to the fact that his or her language is bothering you.

Other sample warnings include:

- ■ "I don't appreciate the language you are using now."

- ■ "If you aren't able to talk to me without swearing, I will have to end this call."

- ■ "It sounds like you are too upset to continue discussing this. I will call you back in 30 minutes."

Step 3

If you terminate the call, inform your supervisor immediately. Give your supervisor a briefing on the situation. If your supervisor is not in the office, leave a written account of the conversation. Tell another manager who might receive the call in your supervisor's absence.

Step 4

Calm yourself quickly before picking up the next incoming call.

These strategies work for many service representatives who are "recovering" from a tense call.

♦ Take several slow, deep breaths.

♦ Count to ten slowly.

♦ Stand up and stretch.

The next call will probably be routine and relatively easy to handle.

You've refreshed your thinking about helping the customer feel satisfied after some problem or disappointment with your organization. It's important to start with the caller's feelings and then move to creatively responding to the issues. For the few times when you encounter a truly abusive caller, you know how to handle the call firmly and professionally. Dealing with the challenges of angry and upset callers is a skill-building process. Satisfying upset callers is something to be proud of! Approach the next call with a positive attitude, and you'll be amazed at the outcome!

Start with the caller's feelings and then move to creatively responding to the issues.

Yes, I Can!

Staying in control of your own emotions when dealing with angry callers is the trait of a true telephone service professional. Jot down a message to yourself to help you remember that you are not the real target of the person's anger.

Yes, to keep my cool with a "hot" customer, I can _____

_____

_____

_____

6

Chapter *Seven*

Handling Difficult Telephone Situations Professionally

Chapter Objectives

▶ Know how to handle difficult situations professionally.

▶ Increase your comfort and confidence during stressful calls.

D ifficult situations occur on the telephone from time to time. They often present challenges we are unprepared to address. By thinking about unusually difficult or stressful calls in advance, you can be better prepared to create a positive outcome.

You will find a series of tough situations outlined in this chapter:

◆ Two or more calls come in at once.

◆ The caller is angry about being transferred.

◆ The caller hangs up.

◆ The caller is crying.

◆ The caller speaks another language.

◆ The caller is mentally challenged.

◆ The caller asks for your manager.

◆ The caller threatens you.

As you imagine yourself in situations like these, add your own notes to help you personalize a similar type of call that you may get. *Jot down any ideas that would help you feel better prepared with an appropriate, professional response.*

Remember that 30 seconds on hold is an eternity for the caller.

What if two or more calls are coming in at once?

Stay calm. Tell the caller you are speaking with that you have another call. *Ask* if he or she can hold. If the caller cannot hold, ask for a phone number so you can call right back. Then, pick up the next line that is ringing. Use the full greeting you usually use except for the "How may I help you?" Substitute "Could you please hold?" If you have a third line ringing, answer it the same way you answered the second call.

Remember that 30 seconds on hold is an eternity for the caller. Reconnect with your original caller first. If that call is going to be lengthy, ask him or her to hold again. Go back to callers two and three and thank them for being patient. Ask for phone numbers so you can call them back.

What if the caller is angry about being transferred or being put on hold?

You have an instant opportunity to change a negative into a positive. Respond sincerely with a brief, blameless apology. Follow that enthusiastically with an offer to help. Your greeting may include, "I'm really sorry for the inconvenience. I know your time is valuable. Now that you have my full attention, how may I help you?"

Don't use this type of opportunity to ask open-ended questions about the caller's feelings or concerns. Help him or her get down to business, and prove that you can efficiently and accurately address the reason for the call.

7

What if the caller hangs up on me?

If the conversation was becoming emotional, the caller could have disconnected intentionally. If it appears to be sudden and unintentional, it is the caller's option to call back.

Tell your manager about the conversation. If you know with whom you were speaking, offer to call back. Be prepared with a blameless apology unless you are specifically aware of something you said that was inappropriate. If that's the case, apologize sincerely and ask how you can help now.

Always let your manager know when a caller disconnects. It could signal a problem with your phone system or the company's service strategies.

_____

_____

What if the caller is crying?

Use empathy. Slow your pace. Restate your willingness to help. You might say, "It's okay. Take your time." If the caller is unable to speak, ask if you can call back in 30 minutes.

_____

_____

Develop internal procedures for transferring a non-English-speaking customer to someone who is fluent in one or more languages.

What if the caller speaks another language?

Try to anticipate language issues in advance. Develop internal procedures for transferring a non-English-speaking customer to someone who is fluent in one or more languages. If this occurs frequently, you may want to record a specific message that you can access for callers instructing them how to proceed. In some communities, interpretation services can be arranged via conference calls.

People speaking different languages will often increase their volume. Be aware of your tone and volume. Keep your tone positive and your volume low. Try simple phrases or explanations.

_____

_____

What if the caller is mentally challenged?

Customers, regardless of the challenges they present, deserve and want our courteous and respectful attention. Gear your thinking and language to an appropriate level as you offer explanations of services or products. Be careful not to sound condescending. Ask questions that focus on your most critical information needs. Keep your tone positive, and clearly communicate without using any technical terms or industry jargon.

Summarize the call to check for agreement before you close the conversation.

Gear your thinking and language to an appropriate level as you offer explanations of services or products.

What if the caller asks for my manager?

Take responsibility for as much of the call as possible. Try to find out what the issue is so you can attempt to address it yourself. If the caller insists on speaking to your manager, ask if he or she can hold while you transfer the call. Briefly tell your manager about the situation before you complete the transfer. If your manager is unavailable, suggest a time when the caller could reach him or her, and offer to leave a message.

7

What if the caller threatens me?

Check with your manager about company procedures in these rare situations. Follow all guidelines created by management to ensure that you are responding appropriately for your organization. If no guidelines exist, use these to frame your response.

Remember that you are representing the company and that the threat is not directed at you personally. That should help you stay calm. Think before you speak. Use a clear message to communicate that you won't tolerate that type of language. You might say, "When you speak to me that way, it's impossible to do business with you. I'm terminating this call now."

Chapter *Eight*

Setting Goals for Better Telephone Service

Chapter Objectives

▶ Use a self-assessment to set reasonable goals.

▶ Monitor yourself for consistently excellent service.

▶ Plan how you will celebrate your successes.

I magine that all of your customers were asked to attend a meeting your company sponsored. They met at a reception in a local hotel. The topic of discussion was the quality of service that *you* conveyed to each of them over the telephone.

Would you be proud of your customers' assessment of your telephone-service skills?

What do you think they would say? Would you be proud of their assessment? Would you want your supervisor, coworkers, or family there to hear their comments?

Turn back to the self-assessment that you completed at the beginning of this book. Circle the questions you answered as 4s and 5s. Read each statement and underline key words. These represent your customer service strengths now. *Keep up the good work in those areas.*

Now choose the items that you scored the lowest—possibly a 1 or 2. Use the **SMART** goal-setting technique to realize your service potential on these items.

SMART goals help you move forward to increasingly sophisticated customer service. **SMART** goals include five components.

S Specific
M Measurable
A Attainable
R Realistic
T Time-limited

Using your self-assessment, write a **SMART** goal for three of the most important improvements you want to make in your telephone customer service.

1. _____

   _____

2. _____

   _____

3. _____

   _____

The following Action Planner will help you set goals to improve your level of customer service on the phone. Before filling it out, you might first want to make additional copies of the form for future telephone service goals.

8

Telephone Service Action Planner

Describe your current level of customer service on the telephone.

_____

_____

How do you want it to change?

_____

_____

Why?

_____

_____

Set a **SMART** goal related to the first change you will make.

1. **S:** *Specifically*, what will I do differently?

2. **M:** How will I *measure* my work and success?

3. **A:** How do I know it's *attainable?*

4. **R:** How do I know it's *realistic?*

5. **T:** Identify the *time* I will begin this goal.

    month_____ day_____ year_____

When will I assess my progress?

    month_____ day_____ year_____

Identify any resources (people, information, and technology) that can support your success in accomplishing your goal.

1._____ 3._____

2._____ 4._____

Monitoring Your Success

Ask for feedback from those you trust—accept feedback objectively from others. Evaluate yourself continually and reward yourself for your accomplishments. Even 1 and 2 percent improvements add up to incredible service results.

When you keep the basic principles of excellent telephone service on the "tip of your tongue," *you* will represent your company positively and professionally. Now, back to the phones! Your customer service image is "on the line"! Keep them calling!

8

Answers to Selected Exercises

Chapter 2

Take a Moment *(pages 32–33)*

1. "I'm unable to access your file right now. May I call you back?"
2. "I will process your request as soon as possible."
3. "I'd be glad to check on that for you."
4. "She's expected at 9:30. Would you like her to call you, or is there some way I can help?"
5. "Could you please hold?"
6. "I'd be happy to get the answer for you."
7. "I'm unable to access your order right now. Would you like to reorder, or would you prefer that I research it and call you back?"
8. "We appreciate your order. Our processing time is generally 48 hours. Will that work, or would you prefer to have it mailed by express?"
9. "I'm unable to access that part of our computer system at this time. May I take the information and call you back, please?"

Take a Moment *(page 36)*

1. "Good news" opener—B
2. "Bad news" middle—C
3. "Good news" closing—A

Chapter 4

Take a Moment *(page 53)*

1. R (results-oriented)
2. E (expression-oriented)
3. D (detail-oriented)
4. R (results-oriented)
5. E (expression-oriented)
6. RL (relationship-oriented)
7. R (results-oriented)
8. RL (relationship-oriented)

Take a Moment *(page 61)*
1. delighted, wonderful service, met expectations quickly
   "Thank you for calling. We are so pleased that we met your expectations and that you felt we gave you wonderful service. Our staff was delighted to work with you. Even though the work project came up quickly, it seems to have been a good match for both of us."

2. tired, stop work and figure out, come and pick it up
   "I'm sorry this has been an inconvenience for you. It would be a nuisance to have to stop your work and figure out how to get the copier running if it's broken. I'd be tired of that routine too. Could I come out now and pick it up and leave you with an upgraded model at no additional cost?"

3. directly to help injured animals, whole range of services, feel deceived, guarantee
   "Thank you for bringing this to our attention. You were correct in thinking that your donation was targeted directly to help injured animals. That is the most important part of our whole range of services. I certainly don't want you to feel deceived in any way. I can guarantee that your contribution was earmarked strictly to help our injured animals. Would you like me to send you a letter outlining how we have used your funds?"

Take a Moment *(page 64)*
1. frustrating
2. irritating
3. angry
4. frightening
5. upset
6. sadness

NOTES